Credit Secrets

The Ultimate Guide to Repairing and Improving Your Credit Score

HADDEN ALLEN

© **Copyright 2021 by HADDEN ALLEN- All rights reserved.**

This document is geared towards providing exact and reliable information in regards to the topic and issue covered. The publication is sold with the idea that the publisher is not required to render accounting, officially permitted, or otherwise, qualified services. If advice is necessary, legal or professional, a practiced individual in the profession should be ordered.

- From a Declaration of Principles which was accepted and approved equally by a Committee of the American Bar Association and a Committee of Publishers and Associations.

In no way is it legal to reproduce, duplicate, or transmit any part of this document in either electronic means or in printed format. Recording of this publication is strictly prohibited and any storage of this document is not allowed unless with written permission from the publisher. All rights reserved.

The information provided herein is stated to be truthful and consistent, in that any liability, in terms of inattention or otherwise, by any usage or abuse of any policies, processes, or directions contained within is the solitary and utter responsibility of the recipient reader. Under no circumstances will any legal responsibility or blame be held against the publisher for any reparation, damages, or monetary loss due to the information herein, either directly or indirectly.

Respective authors own all copyrights not held by the publisher.

The information herein is offered for informational purposes solely, and is universal as so. The presentation of the information is without contract or any type of guarantee assurance.

The trademarks that are used are without any consent, and the publication of the trademark is without permission or backing by the trademark owner. All trademarks and brands within this book are for clarifying purposes only and are the owned by the owners themselves, not affiliated with this document.

TABLE OF CONTENTS

INTRODUCTION 7

CHAPTER 1- CREDIT SCORES AND HOW THEY WORK? 9
    1.1- What Factors Affect Your Credit Score And How Is It Calculated? 10
    1.2- What's My Credit Score? 12

CHAPTER 2- CREDIT REPORTS 13
    2.1- What composes a credit report? 14
    2.2- The differences between a credit score and a credit report 16

CHAPTER 3- TYPES OF CREDIT SCORES 17
    3.1- What are the different types of credit score models? 17
    3.2- Why do separate credit bureaus offer you different scores? 20
    3.3- How are credit scores calculated? 21

CHAPTER 4- IMPORTANCE OF A GOOD CREDIT SCORE 24
    4.1- Renting a house would be simpler for you. 24
    4.2- You'll receive the cheapest auto and home insurance prices. 25
    4.3- Borrowing money is less expensive. 26
    4.4- You'll be more ready for the future. 27
    4.5- You'll have keys to bonuses and the highest incentives. 27
    4.6- You'll build a solid reputation. 27

CHAPTER 5- WHAT AFFECTS CREDIT SCORES? 31
    5.1- Factors that influence your score 31
    5.2- Account Types That Affect Credit Scores 33
    5.3- What Effect Does Having Several Accounts Have on My Credit Score? ... 34
    5.4- What Factors Can damage Your Credit Score? 35

CHAPTER 6- LESS OBVIOUS THINGS THAT AFFECT YOUR CREDIT SCORE 37
    6.1- Requests for credit limit increases 37
    6.2- Credit cards for businesses 38
    6.3- Medical costs that have not been received 38
    6.4- Mobile payment plan 38
    6.5- Withholding utilities and rent 38
    6.6- Parking tickets that have not been paid 39
    6.7- Library books that are overdue 39
    6.8 Signing a loan as a co-signer 39
    6.9- Personal loans 40
    6.10- Automobile leases and loans 40
    6.11- Mortgage 40

CHAPTER 7- IMPROVING YOUR CREDIT SCORE 41
- 7.1- Verify the accuracy of your credit reports..41
- 7.2- Recognize the Risk Factors 42
- 7.3- Do make for-time payments on the bills. 43
- 7.4- Keep track of how much credit you're utilizing...44
- 7.5- If you don't have a credit card then get one 45
- 7.6- Do all of your rate shopping at the same time 46

CHAPTER 8- BUILD CREDIT FAST 48
- 8.1- Get your credit report in order..48
- 8.2- Make periodic payments...49
- 8.3- Lower the credit-to-debt ratio. 49
- 8.4- Request a credit limit increase. 51
- 8.5- Use "dormant" cards on a regular basis. 52
- 8.6- Pay off the credit cards with the highest balance first................................53
- 8.7- Becoming an authorized user. 53
- 8.8- Make use of a credit card that is secured. 54
- 8.9- Keep your credit cards running? 55
- 8.10- Discover When Your Lender Notes Payment History 55

CHAPTER 9- PAYING OFF DEBTS SMARTLY 57
- 9.1- Types of debt 58
- 9.2- Tips to Pay off Debt...60
- 9.3- How Can I Use the Avalanche Method to Pay Off Debt? 61
- 9.4- How Can I Use the Snowball Strategy to Pay Debt?.................................64
- 9.5- How Can I Use Balance Transfers to Pay off Debt?..................................68
- 9.6- How Can I Use a Personal Loan to Pay Down Credit Card Debt?............70
- 9.7- How Can Debt Settlement Help Me Pay Off Debt? 72
- 9.8- How Can I Get Out of Debt with Bankruptcy?..75

CHAPTER 10- IMPROVING BAD CREDIT 78
- 10.1- Credit Repair as a Do-It-Yourself Project 79
- 10.2-More Options for Obtaining a Free Report...80
- 10.3- Errors on Credit Reports May Be Disputed 83
- 10.4- Sending the Complaint 84
- 10.5- Taking Care of Past Due Accounts 85
- 10.6- Reduce your account balances to a level that is below your limit. 87
- 10.7- High Balances vs Past Due Accounts 88
- 10.8- Getting New Credit..88
- 10.9- Seven Pointers for Credit Repair 90

CHAPTER 11- SECTION 609 92
- 11.1- What Is Section 609, and What Does It Mean?.......................................94

11.2- MUST YOU PAY FOR A 609 CREDIT REPAIR LETTER? 95
BONUS CHAPTER- IMPROVING YOUR FINANCIAL SITUATION **98**
   1. EXAMINE THE CURRENT FINANCIAL SITUATION. 98
   2. SET FINANCIAL OBJECTIVES 99
   3. CREATE A BUDGET 100
   4. DEALING WITH DEBT 101
   5. HAVE THE SPENDING UNDER CONTROL. 102
   6. RESOLVE INCOME ISSUES 103
   7. MAKE PROVISIONS FOR THE UNEXPECTED 104
   8. MAKE A LONG-TERM FINANCIAL STRATEGY. 105
   9. MOTIVATION 105
CONCLUSION **107**

Introduction

A credit score ranges between 300-850 and shows the creditworthiness of a consumer. Larger the score, the stronger a creditworthy candidate. A credit score is determined by the total levels of debt, the number of opened accounts, and history of repayment along with other aspects. Lending institutions use these credit scores to assess the probability of timely repayment.

Credit scores are important for the determination of a finance company to give credit. The FICO credit scoring system is used by a lot of financial companies. The FICO score, which was established in 1989, was the only credit scoring program available at the time. VantageScore was created in 2006 by the three credit bureau agencies (Equifax, TransUnion, and Experian) as an alternate to the FICO rating. Based on the amount of details lenders need and the credit score structure used, both FICO provides various styles of credit scores.

As part of a credit scoring formula, credit utilization or percentage is used of the currently available credit. Closing unused accounts can have a negative impact on an individual's credit score.

The credit score was developed by Fair Isaac, and is utilized by banks. FICO scores have been the most widely used credit score. If you want to enhance your score, pay off debts on time, and maintain a low debt amount.

Chapter 1- Credit Scores And How They Work?

Credit scores are determined by reviewing the credit report and awarding a numerical rating to the details. Your credit background and credit use are shown in this three-digit figure. It also informs lenders of the likelihood of being a credit danger. If you make on-time deposits in the past, for instance, your credit score would possibly rise; however, if you begin delaying card payments, the credit score would likely fall.

It can significantly impact your finances. It is important in the lending decision to give loans. Individuals with a credit score under 640 are assumed to be subprime debtors. The interest rate on subprime mortgages is usually higher than interest from conventional loans. Some borrowers might require smaller repayment terms or co-orders who have lower credit scores.

Alternatively, a credit score of 690 and above is considered to be satisfactory and may outcome in borrowers paying only a little interest over the duration of the term of the loan. A score above 800 is exceptional. While each creditor defines their own range of credit scores, the median FICO range is commonly used:

- Poor: 300-579
- Fair: 580-669
- Good: 670-739

• Very Good: 740-799

Excellent: 800-850

People's credit rating also influences the deposit necessary to acquire a cell phone, TV service, or rent a property. Lenders often check credit ratings when setting interest rates or credit limits on a card.

1.1- What Factors Affect Your Credit Score And How Is It Calculated?

There are 3 main credit report organizations in the U.S.: Experian, Transunion, and Equifax. There are five main components in calculating credit scores by all 3 agencies.

For the Equifax rating:

Payment history contributes 35% to a credit score and shows a person's trustworthiness to return payments on time. Total debt matters for 30% and considers the proportion of available credit of an individual that is presently used by, which is understood as credit utilization. Credit history length affects 15%, as there's more data available to use as a reference.

The kind of credit used amounts for 10% of credit scores if someone has mixed installment credit like revolving credit and car loans. New credit also factors in 10%, and recent applications for additional accounts count as well.

Closing credit cards really will reduce your score.

Instead of destroying them, collect the unneeded cards. Consider placing them in designated envelopes. Go online to verify every one of your cards, make information is correct and they don't have balance. In addition, please ensure that they do not have any autopay settings. Ensure your contact information is in the section where you have alerts. Be on your guard against fraud because you will never be using them. Establish an automatic reminder to follow up on your credit cards once a year to ensure nothing strange has occurred.

The credit score is such a number that really can save or cost you a great deal of cash in your lifespan. Great credit scores can lower your interest rates, which could save you money. But it really is up to yourself, to you, to maintain strong credit, so that you have more chances to borrow.

1.2- What's My Credit Score?

The process is easy, but you will be required to pay a service charge. Experian provided a free FICO credit score in 2020 of your new or existing account if you registered with the corporation. At the time, TransUnion was incurring $16 for a credit score and offered free score monitoring for a month.

You may access your credit reports without charge each year according to federal law, but FICO scores are not supplied free of charge.

Additionally, you can obtain your credit scores sometimes from credit card issuers free of charge. See if your existing card companies will offer it.

Also, you can request your credit score when you're applying for a loan from your lender.

You can get your FICO score from the FICO site by paying their fee. Use your credit card scores to fix errors in your credit.

Chapter 2- Credit Reports

Potential lenders and borrowers use credit reports to help them determine whether or not to lend you money and under what conditions. It's important to review the credit reports on a daily basis and ensure that the details are correct and full.

Credit reports are a description of how you've handled accounts, including the kinds of accounts you've had and how you've paid them off, as well as any other details that the lenders and borrowers report to credit reporting agencies.

Credit reports are used by potential lenders and creditors to determine whether or not to offer credit to you — and under what conditions. Others, like prospective employers or tenants, can reference the credit reports in order to help them determine whether or not to hire you or rent to you. Your credit records can be checked for tax reasons or when you pay for things like phones, electricity, or a cell phone plan.

As a result, it's critical to review your reports on a regular basis and ensure that the details included within are correct and full.

Equifax, TransUnion, and Experian are the 3 credit agencies that issue credit assessments worldwide. Some lenders and borrowers do not respond to all of them, so the credit reports from each may differ.

2.1- What composes a credit report?

The following forms of details can be found in your credit report:

Identifying info

Personal details like your address, name, Social number and birth date are included in this part of your credit report. Your credit report's identification details are not used to determine credit ratings.

Data about your credit account

The categories of accounts (for instance, a credit card, lease, student loan, or auto loan), the day such accounts were issued, the credit cap or loan number, account balances, along with payment history are all documented to the agency by your creditors and lenders. It might not include all of your accounts, as those that have been closed for more than three months or which lenders have failed to notify about.

Inquiries

"Hard" and "soft" inquiries are the two kinds of inquiries.

Checking your own credit records, firms offering you pre-approved packages of insurance, or your existing creditors and lenders doing annual evaluations of your account, all result in "soft" inquiries. Credit ratings are unaffected by soft inquiries. Review your credit reports on a regular basis will help you keep track of your credit cards and spot any inaccuracies or irregular activities that might indicate identity fraud.

When a corporation or person, such as a card company or a debt servicer, reviews your credit report after you apply for credit or even a service – like a loan, a bank card, or a cell phone contract – this is known as a "hard" inquiry. Hard inquiries will last on your credit report for two years and can have a detrimental effect on your credit score, but this can fade over time.

• Bankruptcies

Credit reports have details of bankruptcy public documents, including chapter (a form of bankruptcy) and date of filling.

• Collections accounts

It covers loans that have been signed over to a collection agent when they are past due. This involves accounts with physicians, clinics, banks, department outlets, television operators, and cell phone services, among others.

If you're considering a large buy, such as a vehicle or a condo, you can also update your credit report. When you qualify for the credit, this will help you consider what creditors and lenders can see.

2.2- The differences between a credit score and a credit report

The distinction between a credit report and a credit score is that the latter is a single numerical ranking, while the other is a collection of data that gives you a comprehensive picture of your financial status. They're distinct, but they're related since the score is based on the report. Lenders will use these to determine to choose whether or not to give you credit.

The credit score is significant, but you'll still want your credit reports if you want to look further into the credit and check your past. The first move in improving your credit score is to clear up your credit reports. Correct any inconsistencies and identify the areas that you have to change (such as where the largest remaining balances are). Remember, any positive improvement to credit scores takes some time.

Chapter 3- Types of Credit Scores

Credit scores are divided into many categories.

You're obviously aware that reviewing credit scores on a continuous basis is a good idea, but which type of credit score do you check? Is it enough to check both the VantageScore and FICO credit scores, or is it sufficient to review only one? What's the difference between them, and why there are so many distinct kinds of credit scores anyway?

The FICO score, which was established in 1989, was the only credit scoring program available at the time. VantageScore was created in 2006 by the three credit bureau agencies (Equifax, TransUnion, and Experian) as an alternate to the FICO rating. Based on the amount of details lenders need and the credit score structure used, both FICO provides various styles of credit scores.

What does any of this indicate for you, and also which credit ratings should you be keeping note of? Let's glance at just how credit scores function, the various styles of credit scores, and the differences between FICO and VantageScore.

3.1- What are the different types of credit score models?

VantageScore and FICO are the two most popular rating templates for credit scores. In the context that an individual with a strong FICO score will probably have a strong VantageScore too though, the variations between VantageScore and FICO are small. An individual with a poor credit score according to the FICO model would also have bad credit according to the VantageScore system.

What you should note about the various categories of credit ratings is as follows:

FICO

Isaac and Co produced the FICO score for the first time in the 90s. . As per MyFICO, FICO credit ratings are used by over 90% of top lenders when making financial decisions.

FICO has a wide range of credit ratings. A lender can review your FICO Auto Score if you are applying for a car loan, for example. A lender can check your FICO Bankcard Score if you register for an account. You should sign up with UltraFICO and get your banking activities taken into account in your credit report if you don't have a good credit history.

FICO's credit score models are updated on a daily basis to accommodate market developments and to offer a more detailed view of a person's creditworthiness, but these frameworks can take a while to carry out. The FICO 10 suite, for instance, was recently announced, however, the FICO 8 version is the most commonly adopted credit score.

Vantage Score

In 2006, the three main credit bureaus collaborated to develop the Vantage Score concept. Vantage Score utilizes all of the same variables to calculate the credit score, but it weights them differently.

Your payment background, for example, is the most important aspect impacting your credit score according to the FICO model. The most influential variables in credit scoring, according to VantageScore, are credit card balance and credit usage ratio.

VantageScore, as FICO, changes its credit scoring templates on a regular basis. For context, the VantageScore 4.0, which was released in 2017, utilizes trended data to measure trends in credit behavior over time. FICO Score 10 model also uses trended data, but VantageScore was the first to do so.

The below are the VantageScore credit score ranges:

- Very Poor: 300 to 499

- Poor: 500 to 600

- Fair: 601 to 660

- Good: 661 to 780

- Excellent: 781 to 850

Other models

The credit rating templates VantageScore and FICO aren't the only ones around. Equifax, for instance, has developed its own credit rating model, which utilizes a 280 to 850 credit score system rather than the 300 to 850 scale adopted by the more common VantageScore and FICO versions.

Certain credit score companies have credit scores that seem to be exclusive but are simply copying the VantageScore and FICO versions. So if you inspect someone's TransUnion credit rating, for instance, users actually get a credit score premised on the VantageScore model. Mint, a personal finance software, provides "free credit scores," although these are centered upon the VantageScore model as well—Mint hasn't developed its very own credit rating scheme.

Check the credit score provider's fine print and see whether they use FICO, VantageScore, or another credit scoring standard. Choose credit score companies which use VantageScore or FICO if you want a free credit score.

3.2- Why do separate credit bureaus offer you different scores?

You can receive a different FICO or VantageScore credit score from one Credit Company than the others. If you make a huge payment that consumes a large portion of the usable credit, for instance, your credit rating is likely to suffer before the high debt is paid off. However, it's possible that one credit bureau would lower it more than the other two.

What is the reason for this? Since each credit bureau adds fresh details to the credit file on a regular basis—but the three credit bureaus don't all get the same data at the same time.

So, based about how your financial activity has developed over the past 3 weeks, users can get subtly different results if you evaluate the Equifax credit rating during the first week of a month, the Experian credit rating on the 2nd week of a month, and the TransUnion credit rating on the third 3rd week of a month.

Another explanation you can have different credit ratings from separate credit bureaus: Your credit performance could be impacted when a credit report includes a mistake. Since millions of People have inaccurate details on credit reports, it's a smart idea to check them with each agency on a daily basis and challenge any wrong information you notice.

3.3- How are credit scores calculated?

Credit scores are determined by reviewing the credit report and awarding a numerical rating to the details. Your credit background and credit use are shown in this three-digit figure. It also informs lenders of the likelihood of being a credit danger. If you make on-time deposits in the past, for instance, your credit score would possibly rise; however, if you begin delaying card payments, the credit score would likely fall.

The following is a breakdown of how VantageScore and FICO credit ratings are determined. Notice that FICO assigns a percentage weight to each variable, while VantageScore simply determines which factors have the greatest impact on the score.

Credit score calculation by FICO

- 10 %—credit mix
- 10 %—new credit
- 15 %—length of credit history
- 30 %—amounts owed
- 35 %—payment history

Credit score calculation by VantageScore

- Extremely impactful—total usage of credit, your balance, and the available credit
- Highly impactful—credit mix and experience
- Moderately impactful—payment history
- Less impactful—credit history age

- Less impactful —newly made accounts

Chapter 4- Importance of a Good Credit Score

Why is it essential to have a strong credit score?

Since 2010, the overall FICO score has risen by 14 points, reaching an all-time peak of 703 in 2020.

According to a survey from credit agency Experian, credit ratings have risen for customers of all ages in recent times, from Gen Z to the silent gen (age 74+). The bulk of US citizens currently rate in the "good" or "excellent" scale.

This really is great news in view of the Covid pandemic and its devastating economic effects on the United States, especially because a good credit score will help you conserve money over the long term.

4.1- Renting a house would be simpler for you.

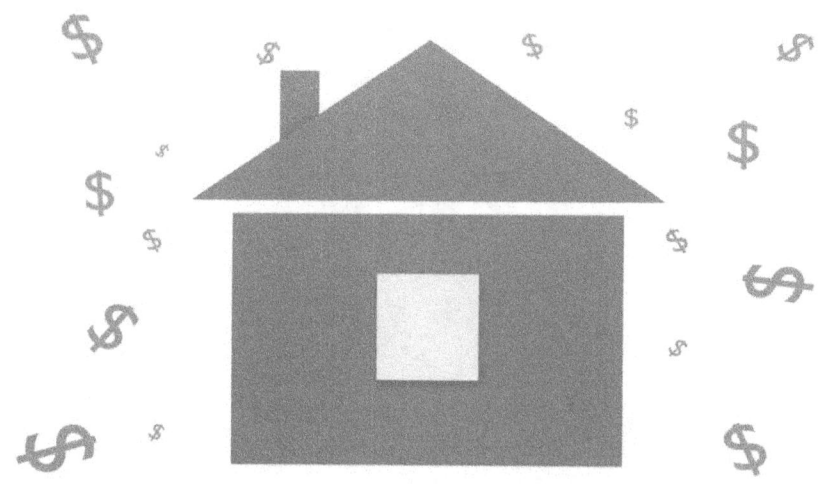

A credit rating of 620 is also the required credit score needed to apply for an apartment, as per Experian. Both VantageScore and FICO's ranking scales classify this as "good credit".

Few landlords and estate firms, on the other hand, are more stringent than most. If you have a credit score of 700 or higher, the rental application phase would be far simpler and your decent credit will make you stick out to prospective landlords.

A decent credit score lies in the following categories, based on the credit scoring used:

- FICO score range: 670-739

- VantageScore ranges from 661-780.

When applying for accommodation, having a decent credit score will prevent you from having to locate a private loan or paying a high-security deposit, as certain landlords require when a prospective resident has less-than-perfect credit.

4.2- You'll receive the cheapest auto and home insurance prices.

A decent credit score will lead to significant savings on your auto and/or house insurance.

Most states in the United States offer credit-based insurance ratings, which allows insurers to determine the liability based upon how you manage your finances.

Other considerations are included when determining the premiums, and insurance firms do not strictly depend on your credit score throughout the underwriting phase. They can't raise your rates, refuse benefits, or void your insurance because of a poor ranking.

However, credit-based ratings provide the most accurate measurement of an owner's vulnerability — and the firm claims that it potentially reduces rates for almost half of its clients.

The most reliable way to see how your credit report will save you money is to get a free estimate from an insurance company.

4.3- Borrowing money is less expensive.

A decent credit score would allow you for low interest on almost every type of loan you may require if you choose to get a car loan, remodel your home, or start a company.

You would most definitely qualify for the cheapest rates and charges for fresh loans and credit lines if you have a good credit score.

In addition, if you're looking for a mortgage, you might save up to 1% in interest. This will result in monthly savings of at minimum $200 every month over the course of a 20-year mortgage on a $200,000 home.

4.4- You'll be more ready for the future.

Having a decent credit score makes you more able to follow lending acceptance requirements and borrow money whenever you need it the most.

If you're in a bind and will need to access a credit card, this will come in handy. You are more likely to be approved for a card with a 0% APR. You will get 0% over the initial 18 months whether you're going through a life-changing event like relocation or a home revamp (then 14.74 percent to 24.74 percent variable APR).

4.5- You'll have keys to bonuses and the highest incentives.

It's no mystery that the best bonus credit cards necessitate excellent credit. There are also other benefits:

You will still take maximum advantage of the latest promotional deals and discount rewards on credit card accounts if you have a decent credit score. "Some higher capital cardholders will get exclusive invites to unique activities, free video entertainment facilities, and even free apparel."

4.6- You'll build a solid reputation.

An individual with a strong credit score does not have to go hard for incentives; in reality, when the credit score demonstrates that you're a reliable creditor, the deals come to you. When you try to refinance outstanding loans, draw out a bank loan, or change to a decent credit card from the new lender, this can come in handy.

Healthy credit patterns track you into the office, even though you don't use credit items. Employers also use consumer's credit reports to make choices on how to recruit, encourage, and reallocate in states that support it, especially if the work entails making high-level economic choices.

The Fair Credit Report Act restricts what your boss will view because they won't be able to see your precise credit score. Employers, on the other hand, may lawfully read the credit report to view things such as available lines of credit (like mortgages), outstanding balances, gross number of car or student loans, previous foreclosures, late or missing deposits, bankruptcies (if there is any), and accounts that have gone to bankruptcy but for this, the employers need your approved consent.

Employers, on the other hand, may lawfully read the credit report to view things such as available lines of credit (like mortgages), outstanding balances, gross number of car or student loans, previous foreclosures, late or missing deposits, bankruptcies (if there is any), and accounts that have gone to bankruptcy but for this, the employers need your approved consent.

Although employers may not be able to see the exact performance, they will be able to see the majority of the details that make up your score.

The most critical practice for a decent credit report is to pay the bills on time.

The most critical practice, if you'd like to create credit and increase your rating so you can enjoy the rewards of good credit, is to pay timely bills.

As per FICO, the single most important element in deciding the credit score is a record of on-time payments. "Anyone who was suffering because of unpaid payments should bring previous-due accounts updated and holding them there.

In conclusion

The quality of your credit score affects almost every aspect of your financial existence, from mortgage and loan approvals to anything as basic as a deal on a new house. A decent credit score will also get you the greatest introductory deals and reward credit cards with VIP benefits like event ticket presales, special activities, and even premium concierge service in certain situations.

Nonprofit financial counseling agencies are a valuable option for anyone who needs assistance with a strategy to get back on course if you really need help to build a good credit rating.

If you're considering credit counseling, find out if it's a for-profit or nonprofit organization, and inquire into the staff's qualifications. If your debts have been sent to collections, you have tax or legal issues, if you need help understanding your legal rights, you can contact a law firm. If you'd like a budgeting strategy, discipline, or incentive to pay stuff off when they're too out of control, a credit advisor or finance coach may be the best option.

When you decide to partner with a mentor or planner, check their credentials to ensure they have the proper education and preparation to assist you in achieving your objectives. The Certified Financial Planner, is the most demanding qualification. CFPs normally receive a charge or commission depending on your deposits.

If you're looking to get out of debts, start with a professional or a nonprofit group, who will never cost you astronomical prices.

Chapter 5- What Affects Credit Scores?

Do you think you'll need a master's degree to work out how your credit rating is affected? The good thing is that you don't have to—really it's very easy.

There are five key criteria used to measure credit scores. Lenders use these ratings to determine how probable you are to repay your mortgage because they are often the determining factor on whether or not you would be approved for a new loan.

Recognizing what causes and forms of accounts impact your credit score allows you the ability to boost it over the duration as your economic profile improves.

5.1- Factors that influence your score

Although - scoring model's exact parameters vary, the following are the most important factors that influence the credit scores.

1. Previous payment record.

Payment history is by far the most significant factor in credit scores, and even a single skipped payment will lower your ranking. When evaluating you for fresh loans, lenders like to see if you can pay back your debts on time. This counts for 35percentage of the FICO ranking and is utilized by the majority of lenders.

2. Amount of debt.

The second most significant element in your credit ratings is your credit utilization, as measured by the credit utilization ratio. Divide the overall revolving credit you're now utilizing by the cumulative of all of the revolving credit caps to get the credit usage percentage. This ratio sees just how much total credit you're using and will show you how dependent on non-cash resources you are. Consuming more than 30 percent of the total usable credit is seen as a warning flag for creditors. Your credit usage makes up 30percent of the FICO® Rating.

3. The length of your credit history.

The length of time you've had credit cards accounts for 15percent of the FICO® Rating. This includes the total age of all the accounts, the date of your earliest credit account, and the date of the latest credit account. The further your credit background, the better your credit score would be.

4. The credit mix.

Top credit score holders also have a broad credit portfolio, which could include an auto loan, bank card, personal loan, lease, or other credit items. Credit scoring algorithms look at the different kinds of accounts you possess and how much of them you have to determine how effectively you handle a variety of credit items. Your FICO® Rating is based on your credit mix, which factors for 10percent of your total score.

New Credit. Your FICO® Rating is based on the amount of credit accounts you have opened recently, along with the quantity of hard inquiries lenders create when applying for credit. Many accounts or requests may mean a higher level of risk, which can lower your credit score.

5.2- Account Types That Affect Credit Scores

Revolving credit and Installment loans are the two forms of lending that typically appear in credit reports. Installment and revolving accounts are critical for determining credit ratings because they maintain track of the loan and payment histories.

• Installment credit refers to loans in which you repay a certain sum and plan to make recurring payments against the total balance before the debt is paid off. These accounts include personal loans, mortgages, and student loans.

• Credit cards are often synonymous with revolving credit, although certain forms of home equity loans may still fall under this category. You have a credit cap for revolving accounts and must make at the least a minimum amount of monthly payments based on how much credit is used by you. Revolving credit is a form of credit that fluctuates and doesn't usually have a set duration.

5.3- What Effect Does Having Several Accounts Have on My Credit Score?

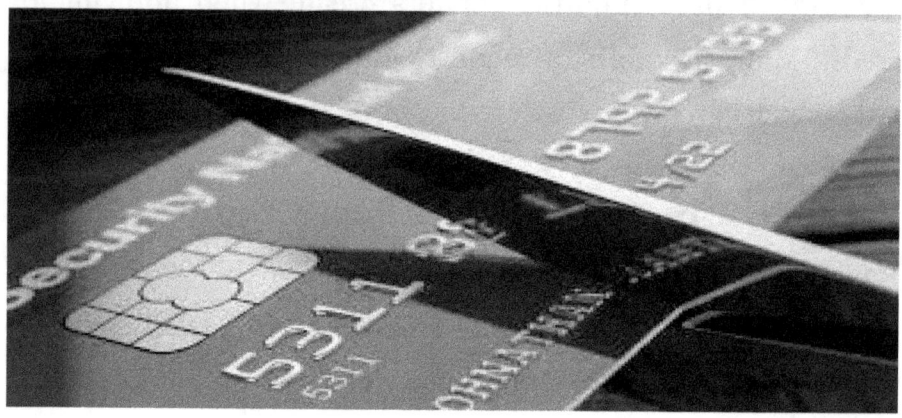

One of the most important criteria used to measure credit scores is credit mix or the variety of credit accounts. It's still very undervalued by customers. Maintaining several credit accounts, like personal loans, mortgages, and credit cards demonstrates to lenders that you can handle multiple forms of debt at once. It also aids them in gaining a better understanding of the financial situation and willingness to repay debt.

Although getting a less varied credit portfolio won't actually lower your ratings, the more forms of credit you have, the stronger (if you make timely payments). Your credit mix contributes to 10percentage points of your FICO® Performance which may be a deciding factor in achieving a high score.

Is it true that service accounts have an effect on my credit score?

Phone and utility bills, for example, are not always listed on the credit report. Previously, the only reason a service account might affect your credit rating was if you did not pay the bill and it was sent to a collection agency.

However, everything is evolving. Experian Boost, a groundbreaking new product, also enables consumers to receive compensation for timely utility and telecom payments.

Experian Boost works immediately, enabling consumers with qualifying purchase histories to see an improvement in their FICO Rating in moments. It is now the only way to obtain credit for energy and telephone fees.

Users will link their accounts to the latest portal to track down utility bills. The customer can get a revised FICO® Score immediately after verifying the data and confirming that they want it attached to their credit sheet. Late energy and telephone fees have little bearing on your Boost rating but keep in mind that if the account is placed in collections as a result of nonpayment, it can appear on your credit record for seven years.

5.4- What Factors Can damage Your Credit Score?

As previously stated, some key aspects of your credit report have a significant effect on your credit rating, either favorably or negatively. The following typical behaviors will negatively impact your credit score:

• Payments that are not received. One of the most critical facets of your FICO® Rating is payment background, and even one 20-day delayed payment may have a detrimental effect.

• Using an excessive amount of usable credit. Creditors can see high credit usage as a sign that you're overly reliant on credit. Lenders want loan usage of less than 30%, and less than 10percent is even cooler. This ratio is responsible for 30percent of your FICO Rating.

• Applying for a large amount of credit in a limited period of time. A hard query is registered in your credit profile any time an investor demands your credit records in order to make a lending decision. These questions remain in your account for two years which may trigger a temporary drop in your credit score. The amount of hard inquiries is used by lenders to determine how often new credit you are asking. A high number of credit requests in a short amount of time may indicate that you are in financial distress or that you are being refused new credit.

• Defaulted accounts. Bankruptcy, repossession, Foreclosure, charge-offs, and settled accounts are examples of unfavorable account records that may appear in the credit report. These will have a long-term negative impact on your credit, perhaps up to 10 years.

Chapter 6- Less obvious things that affect your credit score

Credit scores offer lenders a glimpse at your financial background by evaluating five key indicators, but there's a lot more to the crucial three-digit figure.

You probably also realize how critical it is to pay bills timely, sustain a low debt-to-available credit ratio (nicknamed utilization rate), and have a lengthy history of good credit. You should also be conscious that using a varied mix of payment items and limiting new credit inquiries are beneficial.

However, certain less evident circumstances, such as missing books from the library and deferred parking fines, may have an effect on your credit.

We'll go into these two unexpected cases, as well as ten other little-known factors that may affect your credit score, in the sections below.

6.1- Requests for credit limit increases

Your card issuer can conduct a hard pull on your credit if you demand a credit limit raise. This will lower your credit rating momentarily by a few numbers. There are occasions, though, where credit limit demands have little impact on your credit score, such as when your provider does a soft pull or activates an automatic raise.

6.2- Credit cards for businesses

The behavior you do with your business credit card can have an impact on your personal credit rating whether you're a small businessman or worker. The main account manager, who is also the business owner, bears the most responsibility and, as a result, the most damage to the personal credit.

6.3- Medical costs that have not been received

The most significant element in your credit report is your payment background, which includes more than just your loan and credit card bills. For a certain amount of time, all outstanding medical expenses can be referred to debt collection companies.

6.4- Mobile payment plan

Installment loans, like phone payment contracts, will show up on the credit report and negatively impact your credit rating. So, if you really want the new iPhone and choose a two-year installment plan that is manageable, remember to keep up with your monthly payments.

6.5- Withholding utilities and rent

If you withhold utilities or rent, or if you breach a contract without payment of the lease-break charge, your failure to pay can be disclosed to credit reporting agencies, resulting in a detrimental impact on your score. Landlords and energy providers don't usually disclose your payment records to credit reporting agencies, although they will report outstanding bills.

6.6- Parking tickets that have not been paid

Unpaid fines, licenses, taxes, and general charges, including unpaid tickets, will all harm your credit rating in the long run. Your fare will be submitted to collections if you do not pay it on the deadline.

6.7- Library books that are overdue

You may be surprised to learn that if you return a book at the library overdue and also don't pay the fee, the library can submit your details to collections.

6.8 Signing a loan as a co-signer

Consider co-signing with a close relative or acquaintance who wants assistance getting a loan or obtaining a credit card. This, though, may have three consequences for your credit:

1. The credit report can show a new inquiry.

2. The usage rate is influenced by the amount of money in your account or the value of the loan.

3. Finally, any missing payments will appear in the credit report.

The amount of a student loan and new inquiry show on your credit report in the same way as co-signing a loan would. Your payment background also has an effect on your credit scores.

6.9- Personal loans

A loan, like such a student loan, has an effect on your credit. The credit reporting agencies receive information about the loan inquiry, its duration, and its payment background.

6.10- Automobile leases and loans

At any stage, you can take out a vehicle loan, whether that's a lease or a car loan for purchasing an automobile. The credit report would include the inquiry, the loan amount, and your history of payment.

6.11- Mortgage

Mortgages are definitely the biggest debt you'll ever pull out, and being short on payments will have a significant effect on your credit report.

In conclusion

Sustain a timely payment history and be wary of co-signing credit items, particularly if the partner has poor credit, to prevent detrimental effects on your credit rating.

Chapter 7- Improving Your Credit Score

Enhancing your credit rating

Are you about to apply for a loan or a mortgage and would like to make sure you get the best price? Or maybe you just want to ensure that you are still eligible for the highest reward credit cards? You might just want to start improving your credit rating right away.

Payment history, sums due, credit history length, and other aspects all contribute to the credit score. Although there is no easy cure for a poor credit score in certain situations, there are steps you can do right now and start raising your score.

You will improve your credit rating by following these six moves.

7.1- Verify the accuracy of your credit reports

Your financial record is collected by the three major credit rating services from businesses that you have available accounts. Banks, credit card firms, dealers, vehicle and mortgage providers, and even utility providers are among them. And, although they try hard to gather reliable data, they don't always get it right. According to a survey conducted by the Federal Trade Commission, a 26percent of individuals had a possibly material flaw in their credit reports.

When trying to increase your credit score, the first move is to make sure that all of the accounts and derogatory points in the report belong to you. Federal legislation mandates that the companies include your credit report free of cost every year.

Order your reports and double-check if all is right. If you believe this is wrong, you may file a lawsuit with the credit reporting company as well as the lender or bank that provided the incorrect details.

7.2- Recognize the Risk Factors

You can only get the information when you order your free report through AnnualCreditReport.com. Your real credit ratings are hidden from view. However, buying a complete credit report with ratings may be useful for those who wish to substantially improve their scores.

Along with purchased ratings, TransUnion, Experian, and Equifax have a summary of risk factors. The credit score considers up to 300 potential risks, and understanding what they are can help you identify areas that you can develop.

It's possible that one of the risk factors is a particular account that's affecting your credit rating, or that you've applied for so many credit cards in a limited amount of time. Also, the lack of a mortgage may be a contributing factor. You won't be able to remedy everything—don't purchase a house to improve your score—but you may be able to adjust certain variables.

7.3- Do make for-time payments on the bills.

Send all of your bills on time if you could just do one thing to increase your score. Every single moment.

Your payment background is responsible for 35% of your FICO score. As per Equifax, just one payment which is 30 days old will result in an 80 to 100-point decline in a person's credit score. If the invoice comes upwards of 30 days late, the effect is much greater.

For 7 years, a late bill appears on the credit report. While the negative mark has less of an effect on your total score over time, it still counts.

Place all recurring payments on auto-pay and put payment alerts for other accounts whether you have a missing payment on your ledger or wish to stop jeopardizing your credit rating. This ensures that payment would not fall between the cracks.

7.4- Keep track of how much credit you're utilizing.

After payment background, the sum of debt you have is the second most important element in your credit report. Credit rating services use a factor named "credit usage" rather than a debt-to-income percentage so they don't have your income records. The utilization rate accounts for 30percent of a FICO score.

The sum of debt you have on revolving loan outlets like credit card payments or home loan lines in proportion to your total credit is referred to as utilization. Have a $3,000 credit card balance with a $9,000 limit? Then you'll have a consumption rate of 33%. Your credit usage, both total and per credit source, counts.

It is generally advised to limit credit usage below 30 percent. Those with the best ratings, on the other hand, have a consumption rate of 10percent or fewer.

That being said, there is a snag. Credit balances are normally posted before the due date of your bill. Even though you pay the bill in full every month, the monitoring agencies can always classify you as having a high usage rate.

• Able to pay down revolving credit balances, concentrating first on cards that are near to their cap, will help you keep the credit usage under check.

• If you're a loyal client with a good payment background, you might ask for a credit line boost.

• Making several payments during a billing cycle; making a payment in the middle of the month can reduce the amount recorded to the agencies.

7.5- If you don't have a credit card then get one

The usage of a credit card in an irresponsible manner may have a detrimental impact on your credit report and finances. However, when used appropriately, a credit card may be one of the quickest ways to boost your credit, since it has an effect on the most critical facets of your credit rating.

You establish a consistent financial history by applying for a bank card and paying on time per month. Then, by holding card expenditure down, you will maintain a low consumption level. Credit cards also have a favorable effect on the credit mix along with new user facets.

If you're worried about excessive spending on a credit or debit card, get one with no yearly fee and just use it on a few recurring expenditures. Obtain a credit card, make a minor, annual payment with it, and set that credit card on auto-pay and tuck it away. You won't have to think about making a payment or accruing a large debt, because you'll be developing your credit profile at the same time.

7.6- Do all of your rate shopping at the same time

In the short run, hard credit queries (inquiries for your credit record from lenders while you're shopping for a new loan or asking for a credit card) will hurt your credit rating. Rating firms, on the other hand, have been better at handling responsible borrowers who wish to compare their loan choices.

Prep accordingly to hold the cost shopping within 30 days whether you're looking for a lease, student loan, or car loan. You have to ensure that the inquiry you sent to one prospective lender doesn't affect the score you get from the next one. Inquiries sent 30 days before scoring are ignored by FICO ratings. Please remember that certain earlier scoring models still consider inquiries made during the last fourteen days, and you may not be aware of which rating model your future lender prefers. A smaller retail window is generally cooler.

Credit score models may tell the difference between several requests for a particular borrower versus a search for a large number of new loans over time.

But don't be afraid to browse around for rates when you're concerned with your credit rating. Your score would be minimally affected if you concentrate your shopping window because the aim of a successful score would be to save cash on interest. It's pointless to spend extra in interest to keep a decent credit score.

Changes aren't going to happen overnight.

Although disputing mistakes on your credit file or paying off credit card debt will improve your score in the short run, it is a lengthy operation. It might take some months. Before dramatically adjusting credit ratings, credit rating agencies must see clear, responsible conduct and patterns. Do not give up so quickly.

Maintain a close eye on your credit records, pay all of your payments on schedule, and make progress in eliminating revolving debt. It will take some time but will be worth it.

Chapter 8- Build Credit Fast

If you have a poor credit score, you have a higher chance of improving that quickly than anyone who has a good credit background.

Is a 100-point boost feasible? Lower a person's ranking, the more probable they are to improve by 100 points. "That's basically because there's a lot of room for improvement, and little improvements will lead to big gains.

If you have a better credit score, to begin with, a 100-point increase is unlikely to create a significant impact on the credit items you will get. Simply maintaining your credit will make things simpler by increasing the chances of applying for the best credit card and loan terms.

Here are few tips to help you boost or restore your portfolio quickly:

8.1- Get your credit report in order.

Request a credit check from one of the three major national credit rating agencies at AnnualCreditReport.com before doing something else.

You are eligible for one free credit report every year under the regulation. Be prepared to save it when you make the order.

Examine all about the study after you've received it. Look at certain accounts with late fees or outstanding bills in general. If the details are incorrect, the report should instruct you about how to file a complaint.

Maintaining a clean report is vital for more than just your credit score. It can even have an effect on career opportunities. Until making recruiting choices, several contractors run credit reports.

8.2- Make periodic payments

If you can make tiny purchases during the month, known as micropayments, you can hold your card balances low and boost your credit. Making several purchases over the course of the month affects a credit score aspect known as credit usage. This is another aspect that has a significant impact on the credit report, after payment history.

If you can hold your usage down rather than allowing it to rise when you approach a bill due date, it would immediately help your credit score.

8.3- Lower the credit-to-debt ratio.

Your credit score is determined by a number of variables. Since it is inclusive of a factor that accounts for 30percent of the credit score, your credit usage ratio is a significant statistic. Simply put, credit use is the sum of credit you use divided by the overall credit you have available.

Your credit card utilization is 20% if you paid $10,000 on your accounts and your max credit cap is $50,000. Credit bureaus calculate usage based on your balance statement, but even though you're paying off your payments in full per month, you have utilization.

Using no more than 30 percent of the credit card cap is a common general rule. Many experts recommend holding it below 10% if at all necessary. Most credit cards submit your credit usage to the credit reporting agencies once every month. Your most current statement balance is frequently the amount that appears in your credit report.

Here are three strategies for keeping the credit card usage level under 30%:

• Only charge transactions that are really essential, such as petrol and grocery items or those that win bonus points.

• Use several payment cards to make the transactions.

• Allow extra payments in the billing period for major one-time purchases.

If you aren't planning on having a monthly extra charge, you should easily pay cash on transactions that will bring your balance beyond the 30% mark. If you're planning to make extra charges, make sure they go in until the billing period ends. Your account balance would be smaller as a result.

8.4- Request a credit limit increase.

When your credit cap is increased and your balance remains the same, your average credit usage is reduced, which will help you boost your credit. Call the credit card company to see how you can get a higher balance without the need for a "hard" inquiry, which can lower the credit rating momentarily. You stand a good chance of having a higher cap if your salary has increased and if you've added further years of good credit. Even during the COVID-19 crisis, several issuers could be able to collaborate with you.

Don't do this if you have a struggle with overspending.

The aim is to lower the usage ratio by increasing the threshold on your cards. However, this just benefits you if you don't feel obligated to utilize the newly added credit.

I still don't suggest it if you've skipped payments with the lender or if your credit score is on the decline. Your offer for a credit cap expansion could be interpreted by the lender as a warning that you are about to enter a financial situation and need additional credit. This has actually resulted in a reduction in credit limits in my experience. So, before you apply for a raise, make sure your condition appears secure.

However, if you've been a loyal client and your credit score is in good shape, this is a smart strategy to pursue.

What you have to do is contact the credit card provider to request a credit limit raise. Before you dial, figure out how much you want to spend. Make the figure a little bigger than you intend it to be in case they are compelled to haggle.

8.5- Use "dormant" cards on a regular basis.

You'll also apply for cards with higher perks and interest rates as your credit background improves. Instead of withdrawing the first card, make little payments on it from time to time to keep it running.

Banks are much less inclined to reduce the credit cap or close your card if you leave it working. The credit reporting agencies look at the credit usage ratios in each revolving account and also your total credit utilization ratio.

A reduction in your credit line has an impact on your overall credit usage level.

Shutting an older credit card account will even have a negative impact on your credit rating. If your current card has an annual cost, see if you could somehow change to one that doesn't. You keep track of your account background, which helps to build your credit.

8.6- Pay off the credit cards with the highest balance first.

Work on paying down your credit cards in addition to minimizing your potential expenses. If you have multiple credit cards with balances, concentrate on the one with the largest balance to lower the credit usage ratio.

Paying off your debts will also help you increase your debt-income rate, which isn't a credit score but is seen by many creditors.

8.7- Becoming an authorized user.

Consider requesting whether you should be added as an authorized recipient to one of your friend's or cousin's credit cards if they have a lengthy history of positive credit card usage and a large credit cap. For the credit to change, the account owner does not have to allow you to make use of the card or even inform you of the account details.

This is better if you have a shaky credit history, as the consequences may be serious. It will help you improve your credit score by increasing your credit background and lowering your credit usage.

8.8- Make use of a credit card that is secured.

Using a protected credit card is another option for either starting out with credit or improving your credit. This form of card is secured with a cash deposit, which you pay in advance which is normally equal to your credit cap. You use it much like a regular credit card, and timely purchases benefit the credit score. Choose a protected card that notifies the 3 credit bureaus of your credit operation. Alternative cards that do not need a security deposit may be worth looking at.

8.9- Keep your credit cards running?

If you're trying to improve this situation as quickly as possible, keep in mind that shutting credit cards will make it more difficult. When you close a credit card, the credit cap for that card is removed from the total credit usage calculation, which will result in a lower credit score. Keep the card accessible to use on a regular basis to avoid the issuer closing it.

8.10- Discover When Your Lender Notes Payment History

Inquire with the credit card company on when the balance will be posted to the credit reporting agencies. That day is usually your account's closure day (or the end of the billing period). This is not the same as the "deadline" on the statement.

A "cash usage ratio" is a term used to describe how much credit you have available. It's the difference between how much credit you've used and how much credit you have usable. You have a credit card use percentage on both the total and individual credit cards.

A ratio of just under 30percent —— is ideal. But here's a little secret: Maintain a credit usage level of less than 10% to boost the score faster.

But there's a catch if you pay back your balance each month (which you should), if the deposit arrives after the end of the reporting period, your reported amount will be large, lowering your score so the percentage is bloated.

As a result, settle the bill just before the deadline. Your registered balance would be poor, if not empty, in this case. The FICO formula would then measure your performance based on the lower balance. This improves the consumption level by lowering it.

Chapter 9- Paying Off Debts Smartly

Debt can be a 4-letter term in more respects than one.

This becomes an aberration that threatens your mental and physical wellbeing as it spirals out of reach, whether due to medical costs, shopping trips, or sudden emergencies.

About how daunting it can be, any debt can be tackled in much the same way: one move at a time. Let's talk about how to pay down debt in general — and debt of credit cards in particular — even when it feels unimaginable.

Begin by discovering how debt affects the credit score and also why credit card debt is especially harmful. Alternatively, try the debt avalanche, which is one of our preferred debt-reduction strategies.

9.1- Types of debt

We'll look at two forms of debt: installment and revolving.

Credit cards are the most common source of revolving debt so you can hold a balance each month. You can loan as much credit as you like up to a fixed credit cap, and rates of interest can adjust at any time. On revolving debt, the monthly payment can differ based on the amount you already own.

Mortgages, auto loans, college loans, and personal loans contribute to installment debt. The sum you loan, the rate of interest, and the volume of your monthly bills are usually set at the beginning.

You would make timely contributions on both forms of debt. If you miss payments, your creditor can notify the credit reporting agencies, which will affect your credit for up to seven years. You will also be required to pay fines, which may have little effect on your credit ratings but may be costly nevertheless.

However, apart from the payment history, each form of debt has a distinct impact on your credit. A heavy balance on installment debt, such as student loans and leases, has little effect on your credit.

Revolving debt, on the other hand, is a different story. Carrying large balances on the credit cards relative to the credit limits for month to month would almost certainly have a negative impact on your credit ratings — particularly if you do so with several cards.

Since the amount of available credit you are utilizing — also called credit utilization — plays a big role in determining your credit ratings, it will hurt your credit. Maintaining healthy credit means keeping the credit card balances as minimal as possible. In a perfect world, you'd pay off the whole statement balance per month.

Credit card debt is perhaps the most dangerous kind of debt.

Incredibly low APRs and a glittering credit line will entice you to apply for a credit card. However, the promotional APR deal will expire at some stage. If you don't handle your latest credit card statement well, you will find yourself looking at an enormous pile of debt as it happens.

Interest rates of Credit cards are usually very large, which is why revolving loans can be so daunting. So, if you only pay the minimum amount per month, it would take a long time — potentially decades — to pay the debt. You'll still be paying a great deal of interest throughout that period.

Let's presume you charge 8,000 dollars using a credit card with a 17.5percentage APR, then throw the card in a box and never use it again. If you spend the minimum amount due on your bill per month, it will take about fifteen years to pay down the debt — and it would cost you over $7,000 in additional interest.

9.2- Tips to Pay off Debt

Are you prepared to pay down your debt? The first move is to devise a debt repayment strategy.

If you only possess 1 debt, the plan is straightforward: make the largest monthly contribution you can afford. Wash and loop until it is finished.

However, if you're like the majority of people who are in debt, you have many accounts to keep track of. In any case, you'll need to figure out which debt-reduction strategy fits well for you.

Many people use the debt avalanche and debt snowball tactics popularized by finance expert Dave Ramsey. Here, we'll go through all of these methods, as well as other options.

When you choose to lower the number of interest you pay, we consider utilizing the debt avalanche strategy and it's the easiest way to pay off many credit cards quickly. However, if that approach isn't for you, there are a few others to suggest:

1. Snowball Method

2. Avalanche Method

3. Personal Loans

4. Balance Transfers

5. Bankruptcy

6. Debt Settlement

9.3- How Can I Use the Avalanche Method to Pay Off Debt?

You'll pay down the balances in order with the maximum rate of interest to the least with this debt-reduction technique, also recognized as debt stacking. The below is how it operates:

• Step 1: Spend the bare minimum on any of your accounts.

• Step 2: Transfer as much capital as you can into the account having the most interest rate.

• Step 3: After you've paid off with the largest interest rate, go on to the loan with the next most interest rate and spend as far as you can. Continue this phase until you've paid off all of your debts.

Each cycle you pay an account, you'll have more funds available each month to go into the next. You'll spend less overall and stay out of bankruptcy quicker if you tackle your loans in order of rate of interest.

It can take a while to see something happen, just like an avalanche. Your loans (and the rate of interest you're spending on them) can melt away like a flowing wall of snow until you gather any traction.

Example

Assume you have 4 different debts:

Debt Type	Amount	APR (Interest rate)
Student Loan	25,000 Dollars	5.5%
Auto Loan	15,000 Dollars	4.5%
Credit Card	7,000 Dollars	22.0%
Personal Loan	5,000 Dollars	10.0%

To make use of the debt avalanche process

To make use of the debt avalanche process

2. Always make the appropriate monthly minimum cost for every account.

3. Apply all additional funds to the loan with the maximum interest rate, which in this situation is your credit card.

4. After you've paid down your credit card balance, apply the money you're putting into it into the next highest rate of interest — your personal loan.

5. After that loan is paid down, apply the balance you've been contributing to the student loan payments.

6. After you've paid off the college loans, apply the amount you've been spending for those loans to the car loan contributions.

As a result, you'll pay your balances in the following order:

1st ($7,000) credit card

2nd $5,000 Personal Loan

3. Student loan of $25,000 is available.

4th Vehicle Loan ($15,000)

The Debt Avalanche's Advantages and Disadvantages

The debt avalanche will save you money on interest to help you stay out of debt faster. You'll even get a sense of accomplishment by watching the fastest interest rates vanish first.

As a result, we propose the debt avalanche as a form of debt repayment.

What's the drawback? It could take longer to see results than it did for the debt snowball. And, if you're hoping for a few little victories to keep you going, the next approach may be a great match.

9.4- How Can I Use the Snowball Strategy to Pay Debt?

You'll have to pay your loans in a proportion of smallest to highest balances utilizing the snowball debt strategy. The below is how it operates:

• Step 1: Spend the bare minimum on any of your bills.

• Step 2: Transfer as many funds as you can to the account having the least balance.

• Step 3: After you've paid off the lowest debt, use the funds you were planning to put into it into the next smallest debt. Continue this phase until you've paid off all of your debts.

This strategy is popular since it involves a number of minor victories at the start, which will motivate you to pay off the remainder of your debt. In the debt snowball process, you can even raise your credit ratings faster by lowering the credit usage on separate credit cards and reducing the amount of accounts with unpaid balances.

You attack the lowest balance initially, irrespective of interest rates, in this strategy. After it is paid off, you can concentrate on the deposit with the smallest balance.

Consider a snowball moving down the street: It will suck up ever more snow as it becomes larger. Each debt you pay off earns you more funds to help you pay the next faster. When you pay down the smallest loans first, you'll have more incentive to keep taking off your debt.

Furthermore, the debt snowball approach can have a fast positive effect on your credit rating. You will save money in other aspects as well with better credit.

Example

Take the previous scenario of loans again:

Debt Type	Amount	APR (Interest rate)
Student Loan	25,000 Dollars	5.5%
Auto Loan	15,000 Dollars	4.5%
Credit Card	7,000 Dollars	22.0%
Personal Loan	5,000 Dollars	10.0%

To make use of the debt snowball process, follow these steps:

1. Order the loans from smallest to largest balance.

2. Always meet the required minimum monthly payment due per each account.

3. Put some excess cash against the personal loan, which has the lowest balance.

4. Using the funds you were putting into the personal loan to pay down the next lowest amount — credit card debt — until it's paid off.

5. After you've paid back your credit card, apply the amount you've been spending to your vehicle loan payments.

6. Take the amount you've been spending for the car loan and apply it to the student loan contributions until it's paid off.

By using the debt snowball process, you'll pay your debts in the following order:

1st ($5,000) Personal Loan

2 ($7,000) credit card

3rd Loan for car ($15,000)

4th ($25,000) Student Loan

The Debt Snowball's Advantages and Disadvantages

If you have many small loans to pay back — or if you ever need the incentive to pay off a large amount of debt — the debt snowball might be a reasonable fit. If you have outstanding balances on several credit cards and are unable to apply for a fresh balance credit transfer card or lower-interest personal loan to merge your revolving debt, this could be a viable option.

When you're dealing with a large sum of debt, this approach allows you to see results as soon as possible. You should get rid of the lowest, simplest balance first, which will help you forget about the account.

Reducing the amount of accounts on the credit reports with deferred balances can also improve your credit scores.

The only disadvantage to the snowball approach is that it usually costs more in the long run than the avalanche approach. Since you didn't factor in interest costs, you could wind up paying off high-interest balances eventually. You'll pay more of it in interest fees if you wait longer.

9.5- How Can I Use Balance Transfers to Pay off Debt?

Transferring your credit balance to a new card is an alternative if you're having credit card debt.

For instance, if you have got a high-interest account, you can move the money to a card having a lower rate of interest and pay less interest over time. It's the equivalent of paying off a credit card with another.

• Step 1: Determine which credit cards have a balance for which you are paying interest.

• Step 2: Determine the amount of money you should or wish to transfer.

- Step 3: Register for a fresh balance transfer credit card with a 0% APR on money transfers for a specified period of time (or look for a balance transfer deal on a card that you already possess).

- Step 4: Move the old card's balance (or balances) to the new credit card.

- Step 5: Pay down the new account's balance; aim to do so until the 0% interest period expires.

You'll free up the credit lines on certain cards with a balance transfer, so don't use the freshly available credit to pile up further debt.

The avalanche strategy works better with a low-rate balance transfer card. Because you can choose a balance transfer to down the interest rates on the highest-risk loan wisely, it will give you time to concentrate on the account with the next-highest interest cost. This will help you save money on interest.

Many transfer credit cards also deliver 0% APR for a limited time (usually 6–18 months). You will pay down your credit balance without risking any interest rates if you take advantage of a 0% APR discount.

Assume you owe $6,000 on a credit card for an 18% APR. You could move the balance to a card with a 0% APR over the first 12 months. You'd also save greater than $600 interest if you paid off the loan during that period.

A hidden tip

According to the findings of a 2020 Credit Insider poll, 78 percent of American adults who have done a balance transfer believe that it was beneficial. They are a useful workaround if you will adhere to a strict payoff plan, but they are not for all.

Note: You'll almost certainly have to accept a balance transfer charge, so do the math and scan the fine print ahead of time. Balance transfers of 0% APR and also no balance transfer charges are available on several credit cards.

You may be eligible to apply for a nice balance transfer offer if you're at least adequate credit.

9.6- How Can I Use a Personal Loan to Pay Down Credit Card Debt?

The best banking plan is to pay down credit card debt completely. However, if you're in so much credit card debt that you can't afford to write a huge check and the debt avalanche process is too daunting or sluggish to handle, it's time to think of another option.

Paying off several cards (and documents, and due dates) with a low-rate personal loan may be a smart choice in cases when you have several separate cards (and due dates along with statements).

- Step 1: Do some homework on various loan suppliers to see what terms and fees you are likely to receive. A restructuring loan might be a smart deal if you can get a cheaper rate and pay lower fees than you do currently.

- Step 2: Submit an application for a personal loan through your preferred lender. You will be required to include credit card details such that the loan lender may make direct payments to the card issuers. In certain situations, they'll deposit the funds into your checking account, so you'll have to pay off the credit cards yourself.

- Phase 3: Repay the personal loan in accordance with the conditions. You'll stay out of debt quicker and save capital if you can spend more than the minimum payment per month.

The following are some of the advantages of taking this path:

- Combining card debt with such a personal loan can improve your credit rating: Since a personal loan is indeed an installment loan, the balance-limit ratio isn't as damaging to your credit as revolving accounts (such as credit cards). Paying your card debt via an installment loan will help you improve your credit score dramatically, particularly if you're not using any installment loans on the credit reports currently.

- A personal loan will help you manage your debts: It can help you manage your debts by reducing the number of contributions you have to make every month.

- Using a low-risk mortgage loan to pay down credit card debt will save you money since personal loan rates of interest are also smaller than card rates. If you apply for a lower-interest installment loan, you'll save money in the long run.

Taking out loans to pay down credit debt, on the other hand, may be risky. Otherwise, you risk making the case worse by not adhering to the loan's conditions. If you do not really trust yourselves to use credit properly, don't go this path. Or else, you risk being much more in debt.

Keep the following points in mind if you're using the strategy:

1. Eave credit cards opened: If the cards you pay off have monthly fees you may not want to bear, don't shut them. Keep them accessible to help you make the most of your utilization.

2. Reduce your spending habits: Don't use your paid credit cards anymore. If necessary, conceal or break them up.

3. Make timely, monthly installment loan contributions to be a responsible borrower. If you don't, you're just going to make it worse with your credit.

9.7- How Can Debt Settlement Help Me Pay Off Debt?

When you're aiming to get rid of your credit card balance, debt settlement is yet another way to explore. This technique is more effective for those who are (a) still behind in their credit card bills and (b) have the financial means to offer big, one-time compensation to their lenders.

You may either pay your bills on your own or contract a specialist debt management firm to do so for you. If you decide to contract a third party, make sure you do your homework to stop fraudsters and high costs. It's important to note that hiring a firm to do this isn't mandatory, and it might wind up charging you a lot extra.

- Step 1: Assess your loans and assess your willingness to pay them off over time.

- Step 2: Whether you believe your loans are unmanageable and you've determined that bankruptcy is not really the best option, you may try debt restructuring on your own or employ an agency. The worst your case becomes (— for example, more missed payments), the more power you'll have and your creditors can see that you're less able to compensate them in full.

If you decide to do so yourself, have the following in mind:

- Step 3: Approach each creditor to inform them that you are able to resolve the loan with a lower amount than the actual balance owed. Get the first bid as cheap as possible. It's a good idea to raise your money ahead of time because you'll be in a stronger negotiating spot.

• Step 4: Expect a lot of back-and-forth from the creditors. It is possible that the procedure will take time. Don't feel scared to quickly hang up and try again later.

• Step 5: Get the deal in writing after you've reached a compromise you can manage. If you have got the contract in hand, don't exchange any account or payment records.

• Step 6: Settle the accrued debt, preferably with a fraction of the initial amount owed.

If you'd rather deal with a debt settlement firm, you can:

• Step 3: Do some study and compile a short list of debt settlement firms.

• Step 4: Make contact with each organization and ask about their general operation, planned schedule, and fee structure.

• Step 5: After you've found the right organization for you and signed a contract, they'll advise you where to go next. While the mediation firm would generally manage all dealings with the lenders, you would most likely have to deal with asking letters and phone calls from certain creditors for a while.

• Step 6: You will be asked to postpone paying your creditors and now submit deposits to an escrow account through the debt settlement firm. After the creditors offer to negotiate for the below balance, the escrow account can be used to pay the creditors.

• Step 7: If a successful offer is received, the debt management firm can use the money in the escrow system to pay off the lender, preferably at a far lower amount than the initial balance.

Debt settlement is a deal in which a bank, such as a credit card provider or a collection agent, offers to take a percentage sum rather than the entire amount to cover the debt. If you've experienced adversity such as a career loss, medical issues, or divorce, you may be considered. Some creditors, on the other hand, would accept paying debts even though you do not have extraordinary conditions.

This choice is typically possible only when it's become apparent that you've been having trouble paying your bills, such as whether you've been accruing missed payments.

When you pay the debt, you will be able to pay as little as half of the initial balance in some cases. However, you will be required to pay taxes upon the forgiven sum.

However, you will be required to pay taxes upon the forgiven sum.

9.8- How Can I Get Out of Debt with Bankruptcy?

When you've hit the breaking point and don't know what else to do, bankruptcy will have a new start. Nevertheless, bankruptcy should only be seen as a final resort and it may ruin the credit.

While bankruptcy cannot be summed up in a few simple measures, the general procedure is as follows:

- Step 1: Assess your loans and assess your willingness to pay them off over time.

- Step 2: If you believe your finances are unmanageable and you've determined that bankruptcy is the only option, look at local bankruptcy lawyers.

- Step 3: If you've found the correct lawyer, he or she can guide you through the process. You'll need to include detailed details about your loans, credit cards, debts, bank balances, as well as other financial items, as well as specifics regarding your private possessions and property.

- Step 4: Your lawyer can gather your documents and register your bankruptcy with the appropriate authority.

- Step 5: Once you file a Ch. 13 bankruptcy, you'll be required to make regular installments for 3–6 years.

- Step 6: After the bankruptcy is dismissed, the lenders will write off the specified debts, and you will no doubt be liable. Based on the form of bankruptcy, it may be dismissed in as few as 3–4 months (Ch. 7) or as long as 3–6 years (Ch13).

Personal bankruptcy can be divided into two categories:

- Chapter 7, which asks you to give up any of your assets;

- Chapter 13, which helps you to retain your belongings

You cannot take either form of bankruptcy lightly because it is a lengthy and costly procedure that includes counsel and court filing costs. You may also get credit counseling that has been accredited by the Justice Department before applying for bankruptcy. While you can handle the case on your own, it is recommended that you hire an attorney.

Chapter 10- Improving Bad Credit

Repairing a poor credit rating

It is possible to live with poor credit in America today, but it is difficult. Many tasks get more complicated, impractical, or costly when you have bad credit. We have discussed how insurance providers often offer higher interest rates to drivers with worse credit scores.

If you're having new utilities installed under your name, the provider can run a background review to see if you need to make a security deposit.

Banks review credit ratings before granting you a credit or debit card or a loan, as we already know. The number of companies who review your credit is likely to increase rather than decrease as the years pass.

Make an effort to improve the credit score.

Credit repair is essential for saving funds on insurance, investments, and credit cards, but it isn't the only excuse to do so. A higher credit score will lead to new job openings, as well as promotions and bonuses at your current job. Whether you plan to start your own company or just want the peace of mind that comes with ensuring you can take out a loan anytime you need it, you can fix your credit as soon as possible.

10.1- Credit Repair as a Do-It-Yourself Project

You've either seen or heard commercials for credit restoration on TV or the internet. Perhaps you've noticed credit repair billboards on the shoulder of the road. To repair your credit, you don't need to employ a specialist. The reality is there's nothing a credit restoration firm can do for you that you can't do yourself to better your credit. Fix your credit yourself to save money and the inconvenience of hiring a credible firm. The following measures would demonstrate how to do so.

Obtain the Most Up-to-Date Copies of Credit Reports

Before you may begin restoring your credit, you must first determine what needs to be repaired. Your credit history details all of your errors that have resulted in poor credit. Examine your credit report for any derogatory things that could be impacting your credit rating.

You are eligible for free credit reports from any of the three major credit bureaus once a year under federal legislation. Through

Experian, AnnualCreditReport.com, which is managed by Equifax, and TransUnion, offers a free credit check once a year. If necessary, you may also request by mail or telephone.

10.2-More Options for Obtaining a Free Report

Equifax, Experian, and TransUnion also provide free copies of your credit score, with each bureau providing somewhat different ways of accessing your report.

You'll get a fresh free credit check every month once you sign up for an Experian profile.

Similarly, anytime you create a myEquifax plan, you will get six extra credit reports for free per year. To request your free annual report, TransUnion can guide you to AnnualCreditReport.com. If you don't apply for a free or discounted offer, you'll have to pay $11.50 for an extra TransUnion credit report.

In addition, via AnnualCreditReport.com, all three agencies have offered public weekly credit reports accessible until April 2021 to assist all impacted economically by the 2020 crisis. They might even extend it.

If you've been denied payment because of anything in your credit report, if you're on social aid, if you're poor and expect to search for work again, or if you believe you've been a target of credit card abuse or identity fraud, you're still eligible for a free credit report.

Some states have rules that enable you to get a free credit check once a year. The se free credit assessments can be obtained from the credit reporting agencies directly.

Why would you like to get these three credit reports?

Any lenders and creditors can only submit to one of the three credit bureaus. Because credit bureaus don't usually exchange details, each of the records can include different data. When you order all three files, you'll get a full picture of your financial background and would be able to restore your score throughout all three bureaus rather than only one.

Making an additional set of each documentation is a smart practice in case you decide to contest facts. You should give the credit agency a copy of your record and have a version for yourself.

Examine your reports for any mistakes.

Once you've obtained your credit records, go through them thoroughly. Your credit records can be many pages long if you've got a long credit background. Make an effort not to get distracted by the amount of material you're processing. It is indeed a lot to take in, particularly if this is your first time looking at your credit report. Bide your time, and if necessary, check your credit report for many days.

How to Read the Credit Report

Learn what there is to know about each of your reports. And if you bought them from separate bureaus, they'll both look quite familiar. Your unique identification documents, a brief background on any of your records, any things that have been identified in the public record, such as a bankruptcy, and any inquiries that were submitted about your credit report are all included in all credit reports.

Identifying what has to be repaired

The below are the forms of data you'll have to fix:

• Cards that aren't yours, fees which have been falsely declared late, and so forth. • Delinquent accounts which are late paid off, or have been submitted to collections.

• Accounts that have reached their allowance cap

To create a credit repair strategy more quickly, use different colored highlighters for each category of detail. Using various colors saves a lot of time re-reading the credit report or time you're about to make a deposit, contact a trustee, or submit a letter and you'll use a different path with erroneous details than you will with a past-due account.

10.3- Errors on Credit Reports May Be Disputed

You have the ability to challenge any material on your credit file that you think is incorrect, insufficient, or cannot be validated.

You'll get guidance about how to contest credit report facts when you request your credit report. Internet credit reports usually have directions for filing lawsuits online, although you can still file complaints over the telephone or via mail.

The Most Effective Way to Resolve Credit Repair Issues

Although online conflict resolution is also quicker and simpler, it does not leave a trail (you should take pictures). The same may be said about resolving a disagreement over a call.

There are many benefits to submitting your complaints through standard mail. To begin, you may submit evidence that confirms your claim, such as a canceled check that shows you paid on time. Hold a backup of the conflict letter for the records as well.

Finally, you've got evidence of the moment you shipped your dispute with a certified message with a receipt submitted. Since credit agencies have 30–40 days to review and react to your conflict, this is critical.

You should hold a credit report case layout on your machine so you can customize it for various cases and credit agencies because you will be submitting several disputes.

10.4- Sending the Complaint

Provide a copy of the credit report with both the thing you're disputing outlined, as well as a copy of any evidence you got that reinforces your complaint when you submit your dispute.

If you don't include enough details about your disagreement, the credit agency can dismiss it as baseless and refuse to investigate or amend your credit report.

If the dispute is valid, though, the credit bureau may perform an audit, which can be as easy as telling the borrower if the evidence is correct, and respond to you.

Alternatives to Credit Bureau Disputes

You may also refer your complaints to the bank or company that provided the details on your report. They, too, are required by law to review your complaint and delete incorrect, missing, or unverifiable details from your report. 11

After a Dispute, What tends to happen?

If the complaint is accurate, the agency will amend your credit score, notify the other credit agencies, and give you a revised credit report.

If the element isn't deleted from your credit sheet, the report will be revised to reflect your disagreement, and you'll be offered the option to make a personal comment.

Personal statements do not change your credit score, although they do include more information on your dispute anytime a company checks your credit report personally.

10.5- Taking Care of Past Due Accounts

Your payment background has the most effect on your credit report; it accounts for 35percentage points of your total score. Wing to the importance of payment history in determining your credit rating, having many past due balances on your report would have a major negative impact on your score.

It is important to take note of these in order to restore your credit. Your aim is to get all of your past-due accounts listed as "new" or "paying" at the very least.

Bring accounts which are past due although not yet charged-off up to date. One of the poorest account statuses is a charge-off, which occurs while the bill is 3 months past the deadline.

When you pay the whole sum owed, accounts that are overdue but fewer than 3 months past due will be spared from being charged off.

Be aware that the longer you go without paying, the bigger your catch-up charge would be. Call your creditor as soon as possible to see what you should do to move back on track.

They may be able to forgive any late fees or spread out the past due amount over a few installments. Tell them that you're hoping to stop a charge-off, but you'll require some assistance. Your trustee may also agree to re-age the account so that your payments appear recent rather than overdue, but you will have to bargain with your creditors.

Make payments for cards that have already been paid off. A charged-off balance is always your responsibility. Charge-offs harm the credit score less when they become older, but the unpaid debt makes it difficult, if not harder, to get fresh credit and mortgages. Charge-offs must be paid as part of the credit restoration.

If you pay a charge-off in whole, the credit report would reflect that the account balance is 0 dollars and that the account has been settled. From the period of the initial delinquency, the charge-off record will be registered for another seven years. Another way is to resolve charge-offs at a lower amount than the initial balance if the borrower decides to approve the payment and forgive the remaining debt.

The status of the settlement will appear on your credit record for 7 years.

In return for reimbursement, you might be able to persuade the borrower to remove the charge-off label from the credit report, but that's not simple. The most crucial fact is to pay off the charge-off, and a good account label is a nice perk.

Stay on top of collection accounts. When an account has been charged off or has been in arrears for many months, it is referred to a collection agent. Also, accounts which aren't usually included on the credit report may be referred to a collection agent and reported to the credit bureaus.

You can compensate collections in whole and also attempt to get a pay for erasing in the meantime, or you can resolve the transaction for the below amount owed, similar to how you will pay charge-offs. Depending on the initial delinquency, the collection will remain in the credit record for 7 years.

10.6- Reduce your account balances to a level that is below your limit.

The second most important thing that determines your credit score is your credit usage, which is a measure that measures your gross debt to total credit. It accounts for 30percent of your total ranking. The more balance you have, the lower your credit score could be.

Credit cards that are maxed out cost you valuable credit rating points and high fees. Reduce the credit cap on maxed-out cards and strive to pay the balances entirely. Credit balances of just under 30percentage points of the credit cap, ideally less than 10%, have a positive impact on the credit score.

Credit Score and Your Loan Balances

Your debt balances have a similar effect on your credit score. The new loan balance is compared to the initial loan number when calculating the credit score. The higher you're debt balances are compared to the initial loan number, the lower your credit score would be. Pay off credit card balances at first since they have the most effect on your credit rating.

10.7- High Balances vs Past Due Accounts

You'll actually just have a certain sum of money per month to devote to credit repair. As a result, you'll have to plan your spending. Prioritize accounts that are on the verge of being delinquent. Get as many of these profiles up to date as possible, if not all of them. Then plan on paying off your credit card debt. Accounts that have either been paid off or submitted to a collection agent fall under the third category.

10.8- Getting New Credit

Act on having constructive stuff attached to your credit report after you've settled the bad things. Late payments affect your credit score, but on the other hand, timely payments improve your score. It's great if you have any loans that are being posted on the schedule. Maintain a fair balance on your accounts and submit your payments on schedule.

Where Will I Get New Credit?

You may need to create a new account to reassert your credit. Past delinquencies can prevent you from being eligible for a large credit card, so restrict yourself to one or two credit card accounts before the credit rating increases.

Your account requests would be kept to a minimum as a result of this. Any time you apply for credit, a new inquiry is applied to your credit report, and too much of them will damage your credit rating and your potential to get accepted.

If you're turned down for a big credit card, consider applying for a credit card from a retail shop. They're known for accepting candidates with poor or small credit histories. Have you had no success yet? Consider a secured card, which includes a security deposit in exchange for a credit cap. A protected credit card may be used in many places than just a retail card, which makes it more convenient in several respects. Some subprime credit cards are designed to assist borrowers who are rebuilding their credit; but, before requesting, make sure you select valid deals and evaluate fees and rates of interest.

10.9- Seven Pointers for Credit Repair

When you try to improve your credit score, keep these credit restoration ideas in mind.

1. Recover everything you can. Don't make the mistake of sacrificing good-standing accounts with bad-standing accounts. Continue to settle all of your existing accounts on schedule.

2. Spread out the disputes over a period. If you are disputing multiple issues on your credit sheet, just have one dispute per letter and spacing them out. Too many conflicts can cause the creditor to be skeptical and dismiss them as trivial.

3. Use caution when closing credit cards. Shutting a credit card seldom improves the credit score. In reality, ending a credit card account, particularly one with a balance, is much more likely to harm your credit rating.

4. Figure out what factors affect the credit score. Learn what affects your credit score negatively so you can stop committing the same errors.

5. Don't let failures deter you. As you work on your credit, your credit rating can drop suddenly. This doesn't actually imply that you've made a mistake. Your credit score can increase with time as you choose to apply positive details to your credit report.

6. Attend a consumer credit consultation session. Consumer credit assistance is an opportunity for making some progress if your bills are daunting, creditors are unable to negotiate for you, and if you can't manage to make a planar payment on your own.

7. If bankruptcy is unavoidable, file as quickly as possible. Don't spend resources with plans that won't succeed if bankruptcy is the best path to get back on course. Consider if you should apply for bankruptcy sooner rather than later so that you can continue the process to restore your life.

Chapter 11- Section 609

Section 609

Have you ever tried to obtain a loan for accommodation, a vehicle, or other forms of lending just to be turned down due to bad credit? If that's the case, you might not be aware of a powerful credit restoration technique that you haven't tried or even learned of. The 609 Letter of Credit Repair is what it's called.

A 609 credit recovery letter will help you delete "unverifiable" negative points on your credit report, improve your credit rating, and apply for loans that you wouldn't normally be eligible for.

It's also another useful tactic to incorporate into the overall credit management plan.

We'll go into the following points in this article:

• The "Fair Credit Reporting Act" gives you the ability to challenge inaccurate facts on your report.

The FCRA is a federal law that regulates credit reporting.

FCR does not sound exciting, but if you're planning to use the 609 credit recovery strategy, you need to understand what it does and how it impacts you.

Without your consent, credit bureaus will do a variety of things.

They have the ability to gather knowledge on you around your backs, archive it, and even transform it into files that they market to others.

Worse still, you have no choice in all of this.

Credit bureaus, on the other hand, must adhere to their own set of laws. They must, for example, follow the FCRA, Fair Credit Reporting Act.

In the credit world, the FCRA (accentuated FICK-RAH), the only statutory regulation that dictates what credit bureaus may and may not do regarding credit reporting.

The freedom to challenge any material on the credit reports that you believe is erroneous is one of the most valuable protections you have with the FCRA. You may challenge all of the following facts on your reports owing to the FCRA:

• Balances that look off • Dates that appear to be off

• Anything else on your credit report that seems to be incorrect or false

• Anything you'd like to see checked on your credit report

You have the legal right to challenge any facts on your report if you like.

Obviously, trying to dispute a credit report element does not guarantee that it will be deleted, but it does improve the chances.

11.1- What Is Section 609, and What Does It Mean?

Whenever it comes to credit reports, the FCRA is absolutely packed with protections that you (as a customer) can practice. Section 609 of the FCRA addresses a number of these privileges.

However, there is a catch.

The privileges aren't immediately granted to you. If you wish to benefit from the provisions provided by Section 609, you must be vigilant and submit a submission.

A "summary of rights" for customers must be provided with department disclosures, according to the section.

Each of these privileges basically says that a credit union isn't required to erase negative material from the file until it can't be proven.

What exactly does it imply?

You may apply for an object from your credit file to be deleted if it is unverifiable.

The 609 Message

You must compose a letter to be able to acquire the benefit of the 609 account patch.

If you choose to practice some of the privileges mentioned above, you should submit a 609 letter to credit agencies.

While you don't technically have the power to challenge details on your reports under Section 609 of the FCRA, sometimes people add their right to challenge with their Section 609 privileges inside the same letter.

What's the end product of this mix?

It's possible that an unverifiable negative record would be removed from your credit records, resulting in an improvement in your credit rating.

It's important to remember that anything can happen. The other possibility is that the element would be checked as correct, remain in place, and reduce your credit rating.

11.2- Must You Pay For A 609 Credit Repair Letter?

There are three options to explore whether you wish to deliver a 609 letter to a credit bureau.

1. The Do-It-Yourself Approach

There's really nothing wrong with saving money and doing it yourself. If you need a free 609 letter, make sure you perform your homework first and follow up.

If the details you're disputing exists on all three credit reports, you can deliver the letter to all three bureaus once you've sent it.

Certified mail is also a good option.

2. Get a 609 Template Letter from the internet.

On the other side, if you do not mind paying the money, there's really nothing wrong with purchasing a blueprint and using it as a reference for your 609 messages.

Until proceeding with the transaction, double-check that the prototype is appropriate for this form of order.

3. Consult a Credit Repair Expert

If you should plan to employ a professional, do your research first.

A decent place to consider is to see if the corporation is a member of some of the organizations that provide assistance with 609 letters may be valid, although others may not.

It all boils down to personal choice in the end.

How long would it take to repair a credit score using 609?

When you request the removal of one of these labels, credit reporting agencies have a month to investigate.

Once the inquiry is over, you can expect the findings within 5 business days.

Expectations for Credit Repair in 609

Though there is nothing incorrect with practicing your privileges underneath Section 609 of FCRA, and otherwise, you can keep your expectations in check.

Mailing a letter to the bureaus might not always solve all of your credit issues, even though some detrimental accounts are erased from the credit report. If you've made some deletions or not, your credit can need any additional attention. Pay attention to the previous chapters.

Bonus Chapter- Improving Your Financial Situation

If you're drowning in debt or just scraping by, you should be considering how to get your life back on track. It takes considerable time to go back on course, depending on the severity of your financial condition. But don't give up—if you take a few quick moves, you will change your financial condition.

1. Examine the current financial situation.

Until you set a financial target objective, have an honest look at where you are today. This exercise can assist you in determining what, if anything, needs to be changed and developing a strategy to get you to the desired goal.

Evaluating your net worth, which would be equal to your assets minus your liabilities, is a helpful way to see where you are economically.

All of your savings, like bank accounts, bonds, investment funds, retirement scheme assets, and estate, should be written down or entered into a spreadsheet, but really not your house or vehicle unless you want to sell them. Similarly, mention your debts, such as credit debt and other debts, but not the mortgage unless you've already listed your house as an asset.

To calculate your net worth, deduct your liabilities against your savings. Let's hope, it's good. Don't be discouraged if the data isn't as you anticipated; instead, use it as a wake-up alert that you'll need to make long-term improvements to improve your financial position.

2. Set Financial Objectives

When you've determined your present financial condition, you'll need to figure out what you'll be doing. It's critical to have concrete objectives so you know just what you're aiming for and what you'll need to achieve to get there.

If you have nothing or maybe even a negative net worth, which means your liabilities equal or outweigh your income, you might set a target to get out of debts or buy less, as many Westerners do.

If you've concluded that the net worth is favorable but not enough to meet your life aspirations, consider strategies to boost it, such as increasing your savings, being an investor or landlord, or starting your own company. You could have set a goal to retire early if you've just begun your career.

When you've decided on a target, start thinking backward and figure out what you'd like to alter or do in an effort to accomplish it. It's a good idea to write about your target or pick an image that reflects it and display it in your workplace or room or anywhere else so you could see it and be inspired by it on a daily basis.

3. Create a Budget

You won't be able to spot bad financial habits until you have a budget, which is a monthly spending schedule that takes into account your income and expenses.

Begin by making a chart of your profits and expenditures. Examine the expenses over the past few months, or the same month last year, to get a sense of how much you spent in each group. Then deduct your spending from your earnings. If the balance is near zero, choose to reduce your spending or raise your savings. Food and leisure are two popular ways where many citizens will save money.

If the figure is optimistic, make a monthly expenditure budget. For a zero-based plan, for instance, every cent has a meaning, and at the end of the month, there can be no cash available to budget. Alternatively, you might utilize the envelope scheme, dividing the cash into separate envelopes with different expenditures.

Once you've created a budgeting framework, adhere to it with financial tools, a ledger, or pen and paper. You must have the budget to operate for you in hopes for the remainder of the measures to work to change your financial condition. This could take several months of tinkering, but it is essential to financial progress.

4. Dealing with Debt

You must stay out of debts if you'd like to open up the budget and change your financial condition. Write it off as soon as possible, irrespective of how much you owe or how affordable it is; the longer the debt period, the more you would possibly pay in interest rate and overall loan costs. Wave already discussed this in detail in previous chapters.

To begin, make a debt reduction strategy. List the loans in order of maximum interest to lowest rate if you have a ton of high-interest debt, and then start contributing all of the excess capital against the first debt.

If you do have an unstable amount of debts, you might want to start with one with the least balance and work your way up to the ones with exponentially greater balances.

If some of your loans are in collections, you will want to pay them off at first to avoid damaging your reputation and reducing the amount of telephone calls you receive from banks.

5. Have the spending under control.

This action will help you change the spending habits that brought you into debt, adhere to the budget, and save money to pay your debt. To begin, go through your expenditures and look for budget leaks, or issues with your expenditure that aren't readily apparent. After that, come up with solutions to deal with the problems.

For starters, you will discover that you eat out much too much, which can easily add up, particularly if you've got a family. Find strategies to prepare meals ahead of time so that food is served with little preparation time; this can help you close the budget hole and conserve money.

To stop overspending, keep your credit card at your home and either bring a debit card or cash with you while you head out. Examine the expenses for things you don't need and exclude them from the schedule, such as a workout pass or a seldom-used online package. When you put your mind to saving money, you might be shocked by how many you can put together for the long term.

6. Resolve Income Issues

You can find oneself in a financial position where you are just breaking even or spending more than you receive, regardless of your salary. If you are doing, you might be experiencing cash flow problems. It may be a one-time issue, as the need to postpone a transaction every now and again. Alternatively, you could be so enslaved by mortgage obligations that you will be unable to afford basic necessities such as groceries and services on a daily basis.

Determine if you have a revenue problem once you have a budget next to you. If the dilemma is just temporary, you might be able to fix it by taking on two jobs or investing in a revenue-producing asset to augment your main income. If your operating cash issues continue, you will have to undertake more dramatic steps to improve your financial condition, such as paying off your loans faster to decrease long-term expenses, shifting to a lower-cost location, or returning to college to apply for a better-paying career.

7. Make Provisions for the Unexpected

You may avoid financial stress by making plans for unforeseen life events. First, make sure you're covered by the right insurance. Education, renter's/ homeowner's, auto, and life insurance are also included. When you're making ends meet, insurance can sound expensive and wasteful, but an auto crash and its resulting medical expenses will set you back thousands of dollars, wreaking havoc on your finances. When anything bad occurs, insurance will shield you from the worse and provide you with the financial support you require to get through without spending a fortune.

Additionally, provide a cash reserve for emergency savings, which is a savings account that you will use to cover unexpected expenditures. If you lose your work or experience a big emergency, you can save three or six months' worth of living costs.

Begin Saving And cutting down on non-essential purchases will help you from getting further into bankruptcy, you won't be able to significantly improve your financial status until you still find opportunities to save cash every day and budget for future expenditures. One way to make space in the budget for the priorities you set earlier is to spend less on the stuff you use. You can save money on a regular basis by bulk buying, buying secondhand, and using vouchers.

Try setting up a sinking fund to prepare for a potential benefit, such as a deposit for a house, a vehicle, or your kid's college education. This form of fund functions similarly to an emergency fund, although it is used for anticipated rather than unanticipated expenditures. Spend the time and find exactly what you intend to invest, and then adhere to a consistent saving plan to keep on track with your objectives.

8. Make a long-term financial strategy.

When you're saving for immediate expenditures, don't forget to build a long-term investment strategy to support you expand your money and keep going ahead. This should cover retirement planning and investing.

Before you start saving, experts suggest paying down credit card loans and other huge debts with high interest.

However, if you are debt-free, you would more definitely be able to save. It may be beneficial to speak with a financial advisor regarding your priorities and circumstance, as well as offer guidance about the right options for achieving your long-term objectives.

9. Motivation

The more complicated your situation is, the longer it would take to improve it. Given, this may be aggravating when you have to make sacrifices with your life for months or years in order to stay out of bankruptcy and begin moving on to your objectives.

Staying inspired in the transition is crucial to progress. To hold yourself responsible, share your ambitions with friends or relatives, split them down into tiny measures, and congratulate yourself as you reach big milestones. You will strengthen your financial status and feel better about your prospects if you have faith and determination.

Conclusion

Credit scores are important for the determination of a finance company to give credit. The FICO credit scoring system is used by a lot of financial companies. Potential lenders and borrowers use credit reports to help them determine whether or not to lend you money and under what conditions. It's important to review the credit reports on a daily basis and ensure that the details are correct and full.

The quality of your credit score affects almost every aspect of your financial existence, from mortgage and loan approvals to anything as basic as a deal on a new house. A decent credit score will also get you the greatest introductory deals and reward credit cards with VIP benefits like event ticket presales, special activities, and even premium concierge service in certain situations.

If you're drowning in debt or just scraping by, you should be considering how to get your life back on track. It takes considerable time to go back on course, depending on the severity of your financial condition. But don't give up—if you take a few quick moves, you will change your financial condition

Changes aren't going to happen overnight. Maintain a close eye on your credit records, pay all of your payments on schedule, and make progress in eliminating revolving debt. It will take some time but will be worth it.

www.ingramcontent.com/pod-product-compliance
Lightning Source LLC
Chambersburg PA
CBHW070804220526
45466CB00002B/541